The Journey of the Wolf

Katara Wolfe

BookLeaf Publishing

India | USA | UK

Presentation by *BookLeaf Publishing*

Web: www.bookleafpub.com

E-mail: info@bookleafpub.com

ISBN: 9789395890564

First edition 2023

DEDICATION

This book is dedicated to all my loved ones. At the top of that list is me.

PREFACE

This poetry collection has accidentally changed my life. I started the challenge of 21 poems in 21 days as a way to put the poetical things I think in day-to-day life on paper. I would have never guessed that this experience would move me emotionally and that I could create something as beautiful as I feel this collection is. I sat to write in different locations and found myself finding more and more beauty in the world as I wrote each day. There were a lot of poems that didn't make it in. I felt like I was running out of paper. I showed myself how much I had to say. Poetry reveals the truest parts of one's soul and I truly wasn't expecting to go so deep into my own.

This collection came together with the same themes of identity, fairytale royalty and change. There are many forms of poetry and perhaps a number of broken rules and steps towards finding my voice as a poet. It is designed to be read in order but I won't tell you that you can't open a page and find a random poem to read when you want to. I want to thank you the reader for taking the time to read these poems. It's delightful and extremely special to me that these creations are now written in ink.

And So It Is

And so it is,
A Princess begins their journey,
A journey towards what they thought would be
far away lands,
Far away lands and knights in shining armour.
Knights defeating sworn enemies,
Enemies, battles and demons,
Fighting for justice in the lands,
But the journey wasn't like that.
No matter how far she adventured,
The journey was nowhere but inward.

Morning

Good-Morning to those who wake up,
The people that wake up when it is already over.
Good-Morning to those that linger in bed,
The people who sleep until they can no longer.

Good-Morning to those who wake up,
The people that, maybe, do not want to.
Good-Morning to those who wake up when it's dark,
The people that feel like that is their least favourite.

Good-Morning~! I say to the people who made it,
The people who made it to today.

Saturn's Special

Saturn's Rings shining 'round his spheroid,
Raw uncut sparkling diamonds raining divinely
down.

Collecting crystals in a chalice and crushing
fallen diamonds into powder.
Be careful to collect the dust.

Crunching on clear-cut icicles,
While delicately shaving diamonds into the cup,

The tip of my tongue tastes fresh and full of
clarity.

Drinking divine diamond spirits down your
throat,
It fizzles like sherbert.
Swallowing a sparkling glittery carbonated
refreshment,
Falls and flutters through the soul,
As you finish the refreshing rain.

Saturn smiles
His special, they called it,

The chalice of Diamond Rain.

duty

the bins were too full
it's bin day
i tried to fullfil the duty of bringing down the
junk
the bins were t o o   f u ll
as if to say
your capacity is t o o   f u l l
for anything else.
but that's okay,
They will be there another day.

The Tears of a Knight

Princesses shed tears, but I never do.
Sometimes I feel like I'm supposed to,
Because of the things that happen to me
No, a stoic Knight wouldn't dare be that free.

To cry can be worse than suffering scars in
battle,
Slowing down and feeling the burden up the hill.
Distractions disguised as moving forward,
The tears are still there and it is awkward.

I always feel like there are tears behind my eyes,
that won't come out, blocked by pride,
And then I yawn, and one tear comes out,
"No, I am only tired."
She lies eyes full of doubt.

If a Knight hangs upside down,
Will the tears of a Princess finally fall out?

The Wolf and the Prince

The large white wolf sits staring at the cool
moonlight,
Feeling the howl rise in its chest,
Fur softly swaying in the breeze as the river
rinses the sounds down the forest.
A young prince sits staring at the cool
moonlight,
Feeling a sigh deflate his breast.
The wolf and the prince sit alone looking at the
moon,
The moon stares with love for each,
Offering silent wisdom.
As they both stand
to speak to it,
They see one another,
Standing still both staring,

Both thought they were alone.
Time slows in the present moment,
Will one move or will they be here in the time
between seconds?
Both looking at freedom in the other's existence,
The white wolf bares no threat and swiftly turns
and runs down the river
deeper into the forest and the prince runs up the
river towards the castle.
Heading to their respective packs, back home to
the community.
We aren't so different in front of the moon.

We Haven't met yet

I write to you when
we have not even met yet.
The type of love that
is delightfully mundane.
Light blue reminds me of you.

Doubt

dreadful
the doubt in me
frostbitten and shrunken,
I lay in uncertainty and
allow.

Living Lantern

I captured some fairies,
I put them in a bottle,
It's portable light.

Drag Queen's Crown

We all gather with our sketchbooks,
And large clipboards,
Chatting with our wine in waiting.
Are we in the right place?

She steps out, she entered the space with the
grace of a Queen,
Dressed in a royal red dress, with red hair, a
crown that reaches the heavens,
She holds an orb and a sceptre,
Gracefully she arrived,
Ready to be made into art,
The art that she is.

Dreaming about Teeth Falling out

My tooth fell out,
In real life.
The common nightmare,
Did not stay inside
The dream realm.
Imagine waking and flossing
And your tooth chips,
Falls into your hand,
And you can't wake up.
You're already awake!

Tears fell like
A child learning
How to pour juice.
It felt like reality had broken.
The loss of control
That dream journals talk about,
Was occurring in reality,
And the world ended,
For a while.

But then, I got to the dentist
They calmly fixed my tooth.
And sent me on my way.

So one of the worst feelings,
I still came out okay.

The Prince of Melancholy

Desired darkness, and the Prince of Melancholy
Sifts through the forgotten library.
Something muttered near, draws only one ear.
The prince wonders, his head still.
The rays of sun are not present here.
Whispers in the literature
Deliver only light
That wither plants.

The Prince sifts through latté'd pages in search,
Of an answer to a question, he has forgotten.
A large tower of books, soon to topple over,
lies behind him,
As dawn teases the library lilac.
He has been here all night.

The Prince whispers into the dusty spines of the
forgotten books,
For those alluring answers
but…
nothing muttered near.
His pretty head tilted backwards towards the
high library ceiling,
Decorated with dark dreams and a brilliant
collection of bound leather books.

The finest question delicately lingers with
tension.
The sharp edge of an epiphany.

The flickering lick of the lamplight in the corner,
catches the eye of the Prince.
He exhales delicately.
Pondering and analysing all his woes,
Repeatedly.
Perhaps a poem,
A prescription for the soul.

Sighing once more
Oh.
He catches the brief kiss of a smile behind his
cheeks.
He cradles his head in his hands and chuckles.
It is humourous to realise you are melancholy.
The delicious grey comfort,
The sombre sullen grey weight of your limbs,
Feeling beautifully hopeless and cloudy,
It is inviting and he does not want it to leave.
He desires more darkness.
To romanticise the weary.
Yet the burdensome armour the Prince wears
started to fracture.

Be that as it may, it is far more familiar to stay
The Prince of Melancholy.

Arose Like a Princess

I roused to a little tap I heard one morning,
Glancing out the window,
A little black bird gazing at me,
It said Good-Morning!
And flew away.

I heard another tap this morning,
Glancing out the window,
The little black bird gazing at me,
It said Good Morning!
And flew away.

Once is a delight,
but it visited me twice,
I will remember this
for the rest of my life.

Brown Eyed Wolf

When I stare into her eyes
I see chestnuts and leather books,
Chocolate and fine whiskey.
The world is as calm as the soil of the earth in
those eyes,
A deep calm where dark wood tree trunks bare
their structure.
She can stare at me in the sun,
Without squinting one bit.
I stare at her,
Like she hung the Sun in the sky,
The burnt umber glints in her smiling eyes,
She knows that she did.

Leo

Someone as royal as you could be the only one
to hang the sun in the sky.
You can look at your lover like they hung the
moon.
But the sun was hung by you, Darling.

The elusive sunrise

I don't catch the sunrise.
I plan to, I plan to wake up and go see it
I don't
I plan to wake up go see it and go back to bed
I do not wake up,
I woke up all through the night over and over, 3
am, 4 am, 5:40 am
6, 7, 8, 9, am I begrudgingly arose
Missed it again.
Perhaps to me, the beauty of the sunrise is
elevated because it is elusive to me. It avoids
me.
Not a morning person.

25th Anniversary

I grew up
In a few months
I grew up actually, in just 21 days,
My growth was fast, when looked upon through
hindsight,
And feels slow when in prediction of the future.
When I write I grow up,
It slows my inner racing thoughts into a human
condensed form,
And I can fathom it all.

When floating along as a King, a Princess and
the soul,
I am unable to as the Princess, allow myself to
be aware to see the King's wisdom,
When I am caked in the gravity of earth.
When I write, a link between the King and the
Princess is connected.
The wisdom of the King comes in, and my soul
triumphs.

Save Me! I'm the Princess

For a long long time, I have been waiting to be
rescued,
By some magic fortune or my parents revealing
There's some big secret that makes everything
okay.

For a long time, I have wished I was a secret
princess
To be whisked away to another far away land
and taught etiquette
that I already knew, as if in rehearsal of this day
I was waiting for.
It's all misconstrued it's not like a fairytale.
I know nothing would be what like I think it
would be,
No sitting in pretty dresses without worry and
sipping tea.

For a long time, I wished that a teacher would
tell me here is your job,
You've learned all you can and you've finished
your studies,
Here is your entire life planned and it will make
everything okay.

For a long time, I wished for a prince to come
rescue me,
which really is tough to admit see I feel like I'm
supposed to be
this independent, incredible, individual because I
value sovereignty.
So to wish for a prince felt like a step back,
But then I would not have to worry about all the
things you worry about when you
Don't have enough to survive,
and you feel out of control.

For a long long time, I wished to be rescued,
Maybe, I've read too many stories,
Played too many games that all result in
rescuing the princess,
Even though I act like a knight and I don't ask
for help,
Listening to others, helping them and giving
advice instead,
Completing quests.
Sometimes I just want to feel protected.
Save me! I'm the Princess.

My Hero

My Hero

I have struggled through the darkest night,
I have treaded through the deepest snow,
Trekked across the hottest desert.
I have faced aspects and doubts, demons and
fiends,
I have been through it all to get to you.
I will not give up.
No one else has made it this far,
No one else would try this much.

A Knight needs rest too,
I may take a while,
I will keep going.

I push through the thorned vines,
"I've come to rescue you!"
I look closely,
Actually,
I look in the mirrored pool,
Oh of course. Who I came to save,
is me.
M y H e r o!

It Is So

It is so,
A Prince continues the story,
A story towards what they know will be inward,
The journey that was nowhere but inward.
The journey doesn't end here,
It just feels like it does.
It's not written down so did the story continue?
The Prince ran out of pages,
He was running out of paper,
The Prince continues their way as
A sceptre and a King's crown are presented,
now stepping out of the sidelines as a princess or
prince,
a King ready to lead.

The King's Crown

Today I felt the feeling of blithe when I find
things align,
When you're on a train ride and you watch a car
drive at the same speed,
When you crack your back and you feel relief in
your spine,
Watching the sky change colours while sipping
wine,
It's a silent gratitude we all need.

At this time, my life seems to be in serendipity.

When this happens it is delightfully
Surreal and yet this feels like my natural state.
Now I step into the leadership of my own fate,
And the crown that reaches heavens gate,
Is presented with a sceptre.
I am not a Princess.

I am a King.